A Polar Bear and Her Cub

Written by Michèle Dufresne

PIONEER VALLEY EDUCATIONAL PRESS, INC.

I can see a **polar bear**.

I can see it run.

Polar bears can run very fast.

I can see
a polar bear cub.
It is fun to be a cub!

Polar bear cubs stay with their moms for two to three years.

The polar bear mom can see a **fish**.

Yum! Yum!

Polar bears eat seals, fish, birds, and kelp.

The polar bear can dig in the **snow**.

It dug a big **hole**.

A polar bear uses its claws to dig a den in the snow and ice.

I see a polar bear
in the mud.
The polar bear is hot!

A polar bear will dig in the mud to keep cool.

glossary

polar bear

fish

snow

hole